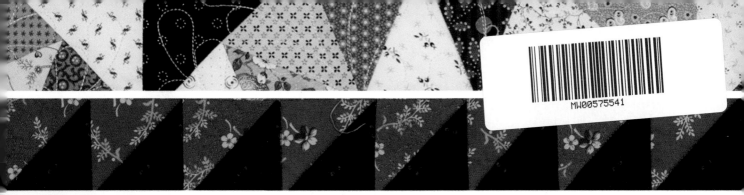

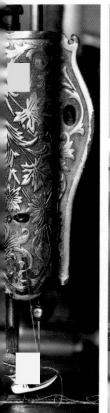

THEN
AND NOW
QUILTS

YESTERDAY'S INSPIRATION -
TODAY'S TECHNIQUES -
TOMORROW'S TREASURES

by Joyce Dean Gieszler

THEN & NOW QUILTS

YESTERDAY'S INSPIRATION – TODAY'S TECHNIQUES – TOMORROW'S TREASURES

by Joyce Dean Gieszler

Editor: Jenifer Dick
Designer: Brian Grubb
Photography: Aaron T. Leimkuehler
Illustration: Lon Eric Craven
Technical Editor: Nan Powell
Photo Editor: Jo Ann Groves

Published by:
Kansas City Star Books
1729 Grand Blvd.
Kansas City, Missouri, USA 64108

First edition, first printing
ISBN: 978-1-61169-134-4

Library of Congress Control Number: 2014942400

Kansas City Star Quilts moves quickly to publicize corrections to our books. You can find corrections at www.KansasCityStarQuilts.com, then click on 'Corrections.'

Printed in the United States of America by Walsworth Publishing Co., Marceline, MO

To order copies, call StarInfo at (816) 234-4473.

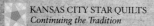

KANSAS CITY STAR QUILTS
Continuing the Tradition

CONTENTS

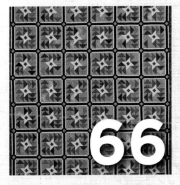

DEDICATION

 To my mother, Madeline Arlene West Dean Hewling (1919-2011). She was a woman who loved easily, angered slowly, forgave quickly and trusted always. Every single person who was a member of our family for any length of time became a member forever. I've never seen people more loyal to a woman than those who loved my mother. I inherited my love of sewing from her and still have the only "quilt" my mother ever made for me. (I use the term quilt loosely in this instance, as it is two colors of faux fur backed by quilted fabric!)

What Mom lacked in quiltmaking, she more than made up for in clothing construction. She made all of my clothes up until high school and still made my coats at that time. Alzheimer's may have robbed her of her memory, but I was always greeted with "Hello, Sweetheart." I'd take quilts over for show and tell every time I finished one, and she would smile sweetly and say "beautiful." Thank you, Mom, for all the lessons you taught me – in front of and away from the sewing machine.

ACKNOWLEDGMENTS

This book would never have been possible without the help and encouragement of friends and family. From my daughter saying, "You've got this, Mom" to my friend Cathy telling me I'm talented and should trust my instincts, I've been surrounded by a group of ardent cheerleaders.

Thank you, Donna di Natale, for seeing potential in my designs. Thank you to my fantastic team at Kansas City Star Quilts – publisher Doug Weaver, editor Jenifer Dick, designer Brian Grubb and Aaron Leimkuehler, Eric Craven, Nan Powell and Jo Ann Groves. Jenifer, you took on a newbie and patiently answered my thousands of questions and led me to a better book. You made my dreams become a reality – a book that is even more beautiful than I had imagined. You took my vision and made it real! I couldn't have done it without your talents, suggestions, help and patience.

I have a fantastic group of quilting friends who encouraged, cajoled, chastised, prodded, applauded and cheered when I needed it. Annette Mandel, Betsy Biller, Cheryl Ferris, Donna Duckett, Donna Pastori, Lynn McCamant and Marge York – I owe you a huge debt for your testing, sewing, companionship, friendship, love and honesty.

Thank you to my family for watching my hobby become a business, a business become a dream. Thanks go to my husband for his patience in my quiltmaking taking over the house at times and for his willingness to visit quilt shops in every state we travel. My son, daughter-in-law and daughter were constant encouragers on this journey. I thank you all!

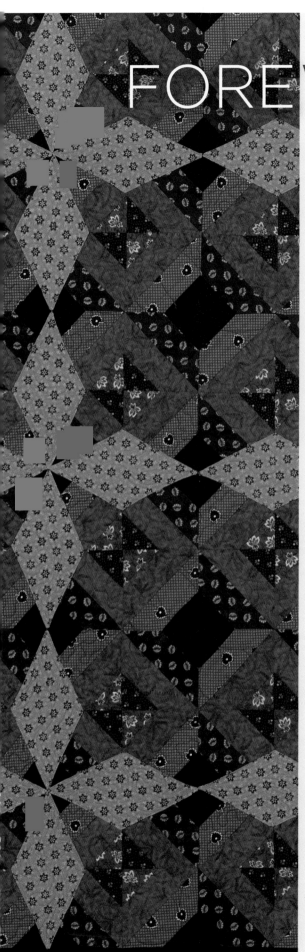

FOREWORD

Art has been part of my life for as long as I can remember. I took every art class available in school and have dabbled in drawing, knitting, jewelry-making and weaving. My sewing career began with tailoring men's suits and sewing a wedding trousseau. My quilting career has evolved from quilts with four or five prints to those with 40 or more! I love traditional patterns and recreating them with modern techniques. I love to study vintage quilts – their color combinations, block construction and borders. Most of the quilts in this book are made with reproduction Civil War fabrics, but as did our ancestors, I added fabric I had on hand when the color was just right.

One of the great joys of quiltmaking for me is helping students recognize their talent and instilling in them a love of quilting. My favorite times are when a student – of any age – insists they cannot be successful. The more skeptical, the better! I haven't met a student yet that couldn't be successful given enough different ways to sew the same unit.

I've always used speed piecing methods for sewing and cutting quilts. I love to chain piece, speed cut and keep moving! I know it's not a race, but I just love to sew! The more quilts, the better. It's not about production, though. For me, the process is as enjoyable as the finished product. I am truly content just sewing, sewing, sewing. I discovered early on that I needed several methods for my quiltmaking to be successful. For example, I don't always use the same method for making half-square triangles. If the finished size is larger than 2", I'm likely to use the Easy Angle ruler and cut strips. If they're smaller than that, I might make them oversized and trim down, or use a bias strip method and cut to size, or even a paper product. In fact, those decisions are some-times based on the contrast of the two fabrics! I'm much more likely to oversize and trim if there is very high contrast as every point is going to really show.

For me, my license plate cover says it all.
Life is Simple. Eat, Sleep, Quilt.

51" square
Finished block: 9"

**Made by
Joyce Dean Gieszler**

**Quilted by
Leanne Reid**

CROSSROADS

My first experience teaching was volunteering at a local alternative school teaching teen moms to make quilts for their babies. Most of these girls were learning how to sew at the same time. I used this 54-40 or Fight block to throw in a little bit of history while they learned to sew an accurate ¼" seam allowance and how to use a simple tool to make star points. Extending the design into the borders was just a bonus.

The 54-40 or Fight block was once published in The Kansas City Star and refers to the political battle between Britain and the United States over the Oregon Territory and what would eventually become the border between Canada and the United States.

FABRIC AND SUPPLIES

1 ⅞ yards white or cream for the background

1 ⅛ yards black print

1 yard red print (includes binding)

¾ yard gold print

½ yard green print

3 ¼ yards backing fabric

Tri-Recs Tool set

CUTTING

Cutting is based on 40" wide fabric. See the Cutting with Specialty Rulers tutorial on page 72 for cutting instructions.

BACKGROUND

- 2 strips – 9 ½" x the width of fabric. Subcut into 12 – 3 ½" x 9 ½" rectangles.
- 4 strips – 3 ½" x the width of fabric. Subcut into 32 – 3 ½" squares and cut 16 triangle shapes using the Tri Tool.
- 6 strips – 2" x the width of fabric
- 10 strips – 1 ½" x the width of fabric

RED

- 6 strips – 2" x the width of fabric
- 2 strips – 1 ½" x the width of fabric
- 6 strips – 2 ¼" x the width of fabric for the binding

CUTTING CONT.

GOLD
- 6 strips – 2" x the width of fabric
- 4 strips – 1 ½" x the width of fabric

GREEN
- 2 strips – 3 ½" x the width of fabric. Subcut into 4 – 3 ½" x 6 ½" rectangles and 12 – 3 ½" squares.
- 2 strips – 2" x the width of fabric

BLACK
- 1 strip – 9 ½" x the width of fabric. Subcut into 12 – 3 ½" x 9 ½" rectangles.
- 4 strips – 3 ½" x the width of fabric. Subcut into 4 – 3 ½" x 12 ½"rectangles. Subcut 32 side triangle shapes using the Rec Tool.
- 8 strips – 1 ½" x the width of fabric

SEWING THE UNITS

TRI-RECS UNITS
With right sides together, lay 1 Rec triangle on the left side of the Tri triangle as shown. Note the alignment of the "magic angle" on the Rec triangle with the bottom of the Tri triangle. Align the long edges as shown and stitch. Press the seam away from the Tri triangle.

MAKE 16
3½"

With right sides together, stitch the second Rec triangle to the right side of the Tri triangle to complete the square. Press the seam away from the Tri triangle. Trim the dog-ears.
Make 16 – 3 ½" units.

FOUR-PATCH UNITS

Stitch the 2" x width of fabric strips together as shown. Press the seams toward the darker color. The strip set should measure 3 ½" wide. Make the number of strip sets as shown in the chart below. Cut into the number of 2" units as shown on the chart.

↓ 2" background

2" gold

COLORS – 2" STRIPS	Strip Sets	2" Cut Units
Background + gold	3	48
Red + background	3	48
Gold + red	2	28
Green + red	1	14
Gold + green	1	14

Make 18   Make 18   Make 12   Make 12   Make 12   Make 2   Make 2

Sew the 2" units together in the colorways as shown in the diagram, pressing the seams in one direction. Make 76 in seven colorways.

RAILS

Stitch the 1 ½" x width of fabric background and black strips together as shown, using 6 background and 3 black strips. Press the seams toward the center. The strip set should measure 3 ½" wide. Make 3 strip sets. Cut into 12 – 9 ½" units as shown.

9½"

NINE-PATCH UNITS

Stitch the remaining 1 ½" x width of fabric strips of fabric together as shown in the chart below. Press the seams toward the darker colors. The strip set should measure 3 ½" wide. Make the number of strip sets shown in the chart. Cut into 1 ½" units as shown on chart.

UNIT NAME	Colors – 1 ½" strips	Number of Strip Sets	Number of 1 ½" Units to Cut
Unit A	Gold + background + red	1	18
Unit B	Background + gold + background	1	9
Unit C	Black + black + gold	1	12
Unit D	Black + gold + background	1	12
Unit E	Black + black + red	1	12

1½"

↑ 1½"
1½"
↓ 1½"

Sew the 1 ½" units together as shown, pressing the seam away from the center.

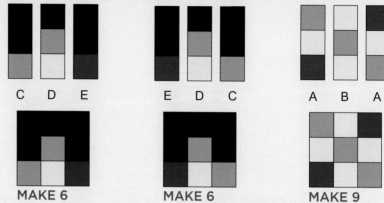

C D E   E D C   A B A

MAKE 6   MAKE 6   MAKE 9

QUILT ASSEMBLY

BLOCKS

I began this process by making my center star blocks and then treated each surrounding area as a border. Lay out the blocks as shown. Sew the blocks together into rows. Press the seams away from the Tri-Recs unit. Press the seams open between the rows. Make 4.

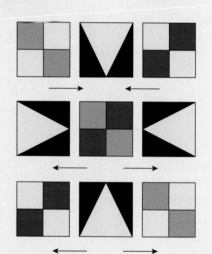

QUILT CENTER

Lay out the 4 center blocks and the sashing blocks that surround them. Sew the blocks together into rows. Press the seams toward the sashing. Press the seams open between the rows.

BORDERS
Lay out the units for each of the borders following the diagrams. Press seams away from the four-patches or nine-patches. Make 2 of each.

FIRST BORDER

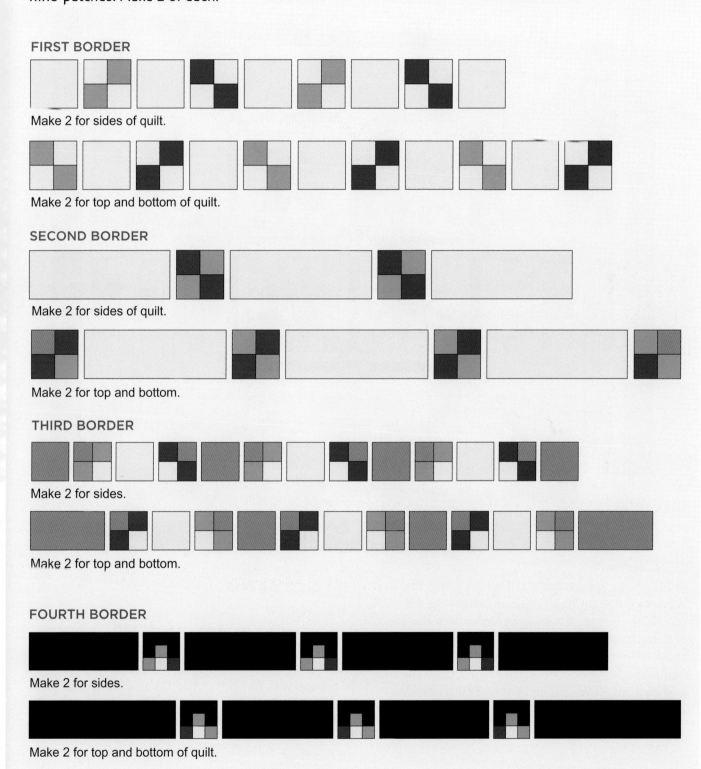

Make 2 for sides of quilt.

Make 2 for top and bottom of quilt.

SECOND BORDER

Make 2 for sides of quilt.

Make 2 for top and bottom.

THIRD BORDER

Make 2 for sides.

Make 2 for top and bottom.

FOURTH BORDER

Make 2 for sides.

Make 2 for top and bottom of quilt.

Referring to the Assembly Diagram, stitch the first borders to the sides of the quilt, pressing the seams away from the quilt center. Stitch the top and bottom borders next, again pressing the seams away from the quilt center. Continue in this manner, adding borders to the sides, then the top and bottom, until you've sewn on all 4 borders.

FINISHING

BACKING
Piece the backing to about 60" x 60".

QUILTING
This top was custom quilted with feathers in the background, diagonal lines in the chains and stippling in the black border.

BINDING
Make about 240"of binding using the red binding strips. See the Binding tutorial on page 75 for instructions.

36" square
Finished block size: 12"

Made by Joyce Dean Gieszler

Quilted by Cheryl Clements Ferris

GRANDMA'S SURPRISE

I've always loved quilts with lots of triangles in them, but was put off by construction methods. Then I had that "aha" moment. If one of my students asked me to help them make a quilt like this, I'd figure out a way to make them successful. As I kept studying the units, I realized you could cut the inner triangle the exact size you need, then cut the outer triangles oversized and trim the whole block at once. Voila! Everything fits together beautifully.

This pattern design is a very traditional one. The Ohio Farmer published 11 quilt patterns in 1894, and one of them was for a kaleidoscope quilt. Maggie Malone's book, "5,500 Quilt Block Designs," calls this block Grandma's Surprise, and this quilt retains that original name.

FABRIC AND SUPPLIES

1 ½ yards assorted medium to dark prints

1 ¼ yards assorted light neutral

1 ¼ yards for backing

⅜ yard dark print for binding

Triangler Ruler or Large Kaleido-Ruler

Note: The ruler must have a blunt tip at the top – the math does not work with rulers with pointy tips.

4½" or 6 ½" Easy Angle ruler

6 ½" ruler

Template plastic to make templates if not using the specialty rulers

Designer's Note: I aim for "controlled chaos" in my scrappy quilts by balancing equal amounts of each color. For example, I planned this quilt using eight colors of print fabrics in a wide variety of black, blue, brown, cheddar/gold, green, pink, purple and red. I tried to ensure that within each colorway there was a variety of medium and dark fabrics. My blues included turquoise, gray-blue, teal, navy and everything in between!

CUTTING

Cutting is based on 40" wide fabric. See the Cutting with Specialty Rulers tutorial on page 72 for cutting instructions.

ASSORTED PRINTS AND NEUTRALS

- 4 ½" x the width of fabric strips. Subcut into 108 print triangles and 108 neutral triangles using the Kaleido-Ruler.

- From the remaining 4 ½" strips, cut 16 print and 20 neutral half-square triangles using the Easy Angle ruler for the block corners.

- 3 ½" x the width of fabric strips. Cut 36 each of print and neutral triangles using the kaleidoscope ruler for the X triangles.

- 4 strips – 2 ¼" x the width of fabric for the binding

Designer's Note: While you can cut 14 triangles from each 4 ½" x 40" strip, I recommend using as large a variety of prints as possible. Consider swapping 4 ½" x 20" strips with your friends so you all have a lot of prints in your quilt.

If you're not using a specialty ruler, cut a template, shown on page 21, from the template plastic. Use a fine point permanent pen and draw in the lines of the X triangle.

SEWING THE BLOCKS

Lay out 1 pyramid of each colorway as shown in the diagram, with an X triangle always in the center. Just think of a buried treasure, where "X" marks the spot. This X triangle makes the whole block work.

On the left pyramid, the X triangle is red, on the right it is a neutral. The pyramid shown on the left is referred to as a neutral pyramid as there are 3 neutrals and only 1 print. Conversely, the pyramid on the right is a print pyramid as there

are 3 prints. The trick to making this block accurately is to cut the outer triangle pieces oversized. Center an X triangle on a left triangle and stitch with right sides together. Press the seam away from the X triangle. Add the right triangle in the same manner. Press the seam away from the X triangle. Trim off the dog ears. Sew the top triangle, pressing the seam away from the X triangle. Don't worry if your triangles don't line up exactly as you're going to trim them. Make 36 neutral and 36 print pyramids.

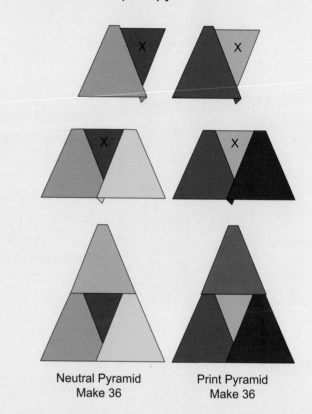

Neutral Pyramid
Make 36

Print Pyramid
Make 36

To speed things up, I chain piece each pyramid. I set up stacks of triangles at my sewing machine and sew all of my X triangles to my left triangles, then press. Next I sew all of my right triangles, press and trim. Finally, I add the top triangles. Once all the pyramids are made, I trim each to size.

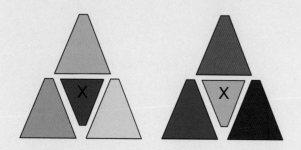

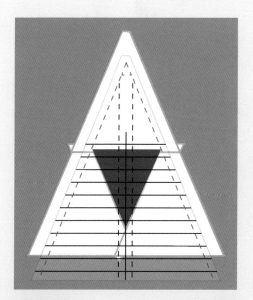

Line up the ruler so that the wide part of the X triangle just touches the diagonal ¼" seam allowance marks on the ruler. Align the center line of the ruler with the point of your X triangle.

Trim the right and left sides and along the top. If you're using the template, line up the X triangle and trim all the way around the template.

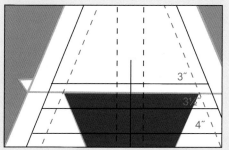

TROUBLESHOOTING TIP: The seam line at the wide part of your X triangle and the horizontal lines on the ruler should be parallel to each other. If not, you may need to go back and correct your last seam.

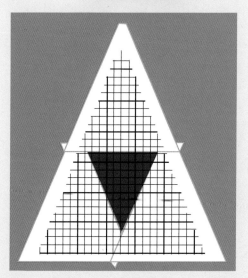

Next, position a 6 ½" square ruler so the 3 ¼" line is aligned on the wide end of the X triangle. The ruler should also align with the top of the pyramid, and the narrow point of the X triangle should be next to the ¼" line of the ruler. Trim off the bottom of your pyramid so it is 6 ½" tall.

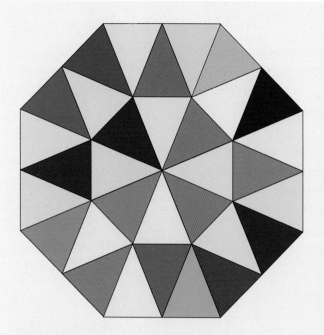

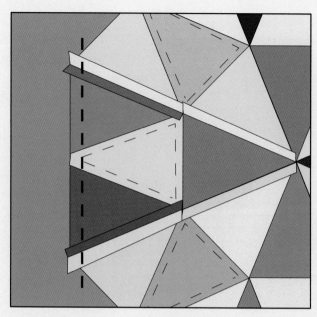

BLOCK ASSEMBLY

Because you've trimmed them after sewing, the units should fit together perfectly. Just to be sure, pin the units together where the seams intersect.

Stitch the seam. Before pressing the seams open, check to be sure you are happy with how your points match. If you're not happy, resew the seam. Sew the pyramids into 36 pairs, then sew the pairs together into 18 halves, then sew the halves together. Press all seams open. Repeat for all 9 blocks.

Stitch the half-square triangles to make corners with the corner piece on the bottom. This helps stabilize the bias of the half-square triangle. Remember that you're sewing to opposite colors – if the triangles of your pyramid are prints, you'll add a neutral triangle to make a corner. Press the seams toward the corner triangle. Repeat on all 4 corners of all 9 blocks. Trim the block to 12 ½". The corners are only oversized by a fraction, so don't be surprised if you don't need to do much trimming! Make 5 blocks with neutral corners and 4 blocks with print corners.

MAKE 5 WITH NEUTRAL CORNERS

MAKE 4 WITH PRINT CORNERS

Lay out your quilt blocks as shown. Sew the blocks together into rows, pressing seams open. Sew the rows together, pressing seams open.

FINISHING

BACKING
Use the 1 ¼ yards backing fabric for backing.

QUILTING
Grandma's Surprise was quilted with cream-colored thread in a Feather Pinwheel 004 pattern by Sweet Dreams Quilts Studio. Refer to the Resources page 79 for contact information.

BINDING
Make about 160" of binding using the dark print strips. See the Binding tutorial on page 75 for instructions.

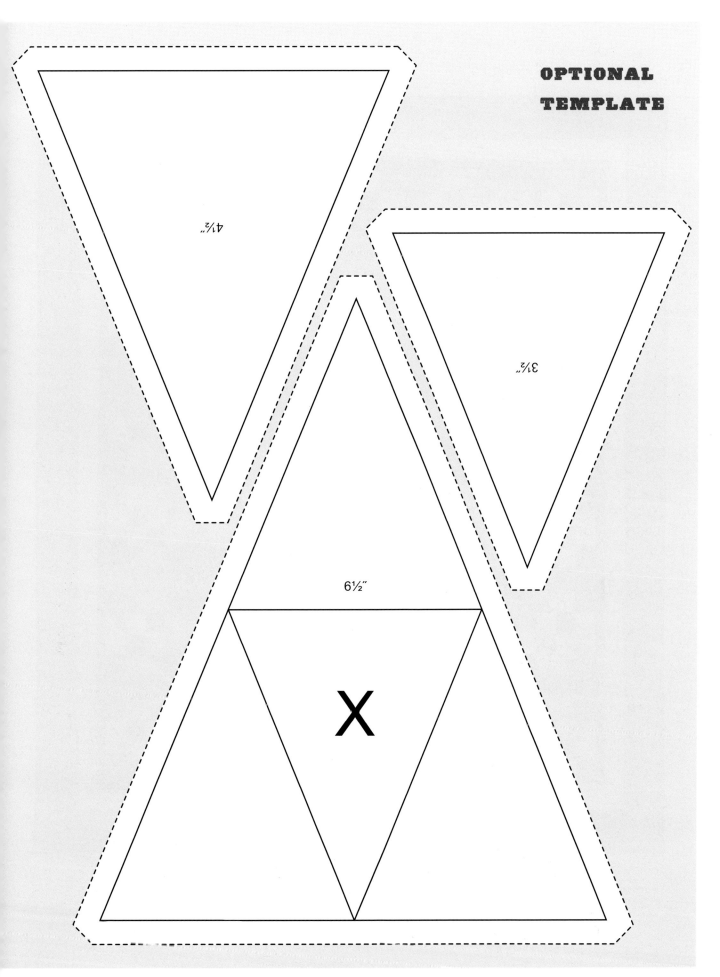

OPTIONAL TEMPLATE

4½″

3½″

6½″

X

64" x 74 1/2"
Finished block size: 8"

Made by
Joyce Dean Gieszler

Quilted by
Leanne Reid

PLUM CINNAMON JAM

I love plum and chocolate and wanted to create a quilt that looks vintage and well-loved using those colors – like those faded brown quilts where you're not sure of the original color of fabric. Each block is made from a different print to increase the scrap feel. It's a great project for a fabric swap among friends. No strip piecing here, just old-fashioned sewing. The "sew, trim, and flip" method is used on a rectangle in place of half-square triangles. The striped fabric enhances the vintage feel, the four borders are treated as one and corners are mitered. My fabrics were a reddish brown and reminded me of the plum jam we made every year.

The block used is a variation of the Road to Oklahoma block published by The Kansas City Star.

FABRIC AND SUPPLIES

⅛ yard each 15 different plum prints

⅛ yard each 15 different brown prints

2 ¼ yards neutral background fabric for blocks and borders

2 ½ yards brown print or narrow stripe. If using a stripe, make sure it runs the length of the fabric.

1 ½ yards dark brown solid for the borders, cornerstones and binding

4 ¾ yards backing fabric

Designer's Note: For the striped borders and sashing to line up properly, they need to be cut identically. Find the section of the stripe you'd like centered on your border. Cut 1 3/4" on both sides of that line for a 3 1/2" wide border.

CUTTING

PLUM PRINTS FOR QUILT BLOCKS
10 – 2 ½" squares from each of 15 different fabrics

BROWN PRINTS FOR QUILT BLOCKS
10 – 2 ½" squares from each of 15 different fabrics

BACKGROUND FOR QUILT BLOCKS AND BORDERS

- 4 strips – 2 ½" x the width of fabric. Subcut into 60 – 2 ½" squares.

- 8 strips – 4 ½" x the width of fabric. Subcut into 120 – 2 ½" x 4 ½" rectangles.

- 9 strips – 2 ½" x the width of fabric for border

CUTTING CONT.

STRIPE FOR SASHING AND BORDER

- 2 strips – 3 ½" wide x 80" long, along the length of the fabric for Border 4 sides

- 2 strips – 3 ½" wide x 70" long, along the length of the fabric for Border 4 top and bottom

From the remaining stripe, cut 49 – 3" x 8 ½" pieces, ensuring that the stripe runs the length of the piece. Be sure to cut the strip as above using the 1 ½" line on your ruler for a 3" wide strip.

BROWN SOLID FOR CORNERSTONES, BORDERS AND BINDING

- 2 strips – 3" x the width of fabric. Subcut into 20 – 3" squares.
- 16 strips – 1 ½" x the width of fabric for the borders
- 8 strips – 2 ¼" x the width of fabric for binding

SEWING THE BLOCKS

For each block you will need:
- 10 – 2 ½" plum or brown print (focal fabric) squares
- 2 – 2 ½" background squares
- 4 – 2 ½" x 4 ½" background rectangles

With right sides together, sew 1 focal square to 1 background square. Press the seam toward the focal fabric. Make 2. Sew as shown to make a four-patch unit. Press the seam open. Make 1 per block.

Draw a diagonal line on the wrong side of 4 – 2 ½" focal fabric squares. With right sides together, place the square on the corner of a 2 ½" x 4 ½" background rectangle. Stitch a threads width away from the drawn line, toward the upper left corner. Cut the seam allowance to ¼" and press the seam away from the rectangle. Make 2. Using the same technique, make 2 units with the focal fabric on the opposite end of the rectangle.

MAKE 1 PER BLOCK
4 ½" UNFINISHED

MAKE 2 PER BLOCK
2 ½" x 4 ½" UNFINISHED

MAKE 2 PER BLOCK
2 ½" x 4 ½" UNFINISHED

Lay out the component parts of the block as shown. Sew into rows, pressing the seams as indicated by the arrows. Sew the rows together, pressing the seams away from the center square. The block should measure 8 ½" square. Make 15 plum and 15 brown print blocks.

ASSEMBLING THE QUILT

Lay out your quilt blocks, sashing and 3" brown solid squares as shown, paying particular attention to the orientation of each block and alternating block colors. The brown blocks "lean" in one direction and the plum blocks "lean" in the opposite direction. Sew the blocks and sashing together into rows. Press the seams toward the sashing strips. Sew the rows together. Press the seams toward the sashing.

BROWN AND
PURPLE
PLUM
CINNAMON JAM
BLOCK
8 ½" UNFINISHED
MAKE 15 EACH

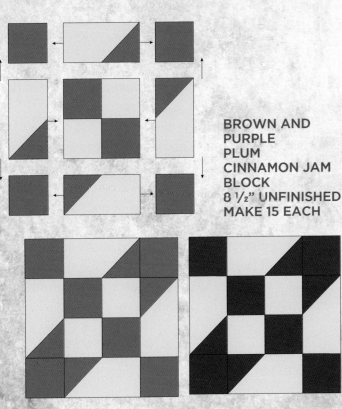

BORDERS

This quilt has 4 borders that will be sewn together and handled as one piece. This will make the borders mitered and give the quilt a framed look.

BORDERS 1 AND 3 Join the 1 ½" strips of brown solid on the diagonal. Check to ensure your seam creates one long length before trimming the seam allowance to ¼". Press the seams open to reduce bulk. Cut 4 strips 70" long and 4 strips 80" long.

BORDER 2 Sew the 2 ½" background strips following the instructions for Borders 1 and 3. Cut 2 strips 70" long and 2 strips 80" long.

BORDER 4 This border uses the stripe fabric already cut lengthwise.

BORDER CONSTRUCTION

Stitch the 70" strips together as shown – brown 1 ½", background 2 ½", brown 1 ½" and stripe 3 ½". Press the seams open. Make 2. In the same manner, stitch the 80" strips together. Press the seams open. Make 2.

BORDER 1
BORDER 2
BORDER 3
BORDER 4

MAKE 2 – 70" LONG
MAKE 2 – 80" LONG

Measure your quilt carefully through the center of the quilt, both length and width.

Calculate one-half of the above measurements. For example, my quilt at this point measured 61" long by 50 ½" wide. So my one-half measurements were 30 ½" and 25 ¼". Yours should be close, but it's okay if they're not the same measurement. Write down your one-half measurements.

Mark the center of the border strips with a pin. Starting at the pin, measure half the length of the quilt along the border (using your one-half length measurement). Mark it with another pin. Repeat to measure and mark the other half.

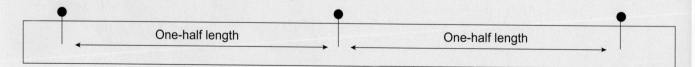

One-half length   One-half length

On the wrong side of the quilt, with a pencil, mark ¼" from both edges at each corner. Your marks will look like an X. Fold the quilt in half lengthwise to find the center. Mark with a pin. With right sides together, pin the side border to the quilt, matching the center pins. The outer pins should align with the edge of the quilt.

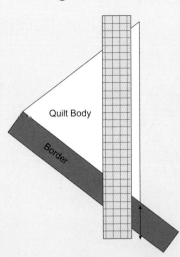

Stitch the border to the quilt, beginning and ending ¼" away from the ends. Backstitch at each end. Repeat for the remaining 3 borders. Press seam toward the border.

Fold the quilt diagonally with right sides together so the right sides of adjacent borders are aligned and the raw edges match. Lay a ruler along the fold line and across the border edges. Draw a line from the end point of the border seam to the outer corner of the border. Pin the seam, then stitch on the line. Backstitch at each end.

Open the quilt to ensure each corner lies flat, it is square and your stripes line up. Trim seam allowance to ¼" and press open.

FINISHING

BACKING
Piece the backing to about 73" x 83".

QUILTED
This top was quilted by Leanne Reid with an allover curly pattern in the blocks, either a spiral or flower in the cornerstones and freehand feathers in the borders.

BINDING
Make about 320" of binding using the brown solid strips. See the Binding tutorial on page 75 for instructions.

73" x 87"
Finished block size: 12 ½"

**Made by
Joyce Dean Gieszler**

**Quilted by
Shawn Priggel**

IOWA SOIL

If you had asked me 10 years ago to make a quilt in only browns, I would have groaned. I just didn't see the beauty and variety that browns could offer. Once the seed was planted, though, I started noticing more and more beautiful brown fabrics. Along the way, our daughter moved to Iowa for undergrad school and ended up staying, working and finishing grad school there. I have two grandmothers born in Iowa, and this quilt, originally designed in indigo, was born. This quilt uses the Tri Recs Tool for making crisp points and a dramatic border.

This quilt block is traditionally known as the Corner Star block according to Maggie Malone's "5,500 Quilt Block Designs." I found references to similar patterns published in the 1930s.

FABRIC AND SUPPLIES

3 ½ yards neutral print for background
2 ¼ yards brown for sashing, borders and binding
20 assorted fat quarters of brown prints for blocks
5 ¼ yards for backing
Tri-Recs Tool

CUTTING

Cutting is based on 40" wide fabric. See the Cutting with Specialty Rulers tutorial on page 72 for cutting instructions.

BACKGROUND
- 4 – 5" x 82" length of fabric strips for the border. From the remaining 20" x 82" piece, cut 160 – 3" squares.
- 1 – 2 ½" strip. Subcut into 12 – 2 ½" squares.
- 5 – 2 ¼" strips. Subcut into 80 – 2 ¼" squares.
- 5 – 4" strips. Subcut into 72 Tri triangles.

BROWN
- 2 – 13" strips. Subcut into 31 – 2 ½" x 13" rectangles.
- 6 – 4" strips. Subcut into 4 – 4" squares, 68 Tri shapes and 4 Rec pairs (be sure to fold the fabric strip right sides together so you have mirrored pairs).
- 9 – 2 ¼" strips for binding

ASSORTED PRINT FAT QUARTERS
From each fat quarter, cut for one block:
- 2 – 5" squares. Cut each square once on the diagonal.
- 2 – 2 ¼" squares
- 1 – 2 ¼" x 5 ¾" rectangle
- 8 pairs of Rec triangles, cut from 1 - 3" x 20" strip. *Note*: Be sure to fold the 3" strip right sides together to end up with mirrored pairs.

SEWING THE BLOCKS

FOR EACH BLOCK YOU WILL NEED:

- 4 – 2 ¼" background squares
- 2 – 2 ¼" print squares
- 1 – 2 ¼" x 5 ¾" rectangle
- 4 triangles cut from 5" squares
- 8 neutral Tri triangles
- 8 pairs print Rec triangles
- 8 – 3" background squares

Sew a 2 ¼" background square to the opposite sides of a 2 ¼" print square. Press the seams toward the brown. Make 2.

Sew these units to opposite sides of the 2 ¼" x 5 ¾" print rectangle. Press the seams toward the rectangle.

Sew a print triangle, cut from the 5" squares, to opposite sides of the block. Press the seams toward the triangle. Repeat for the last two sides.

Square the block to 8". *Note:* See the Squaring a Block or Unit tutorial on page 74 for instructions on squaring up the units.

With right sides together, lay one Rec triangle on the left side of the Tri triangle as shown. Note the alignment of the "magic angle" on the Rec triangle with the bottom of the Tri triangle. Align the long edges as shown and stitch. Press the seam away from the Tri triangle.

With right sides together, stitch the second Rec triangle to the right side of the Tri triangle to complete the square. Press the seam away from the Tri triangle. Trim the dog ears.

Arrange the Tri-Recs units, the center square unit and the 3" background squares as shown. Sew the pieces in the top and bottom rows together, pressing the seams toward the 3" background squares. Sew the side pieces together, pressing the seams toward the 3" background square. Sew the side pieces to the center square unit, pressing the seams toward the center square.

To reduce bulk in the block and allow it to lay flat while pressing, I clipped into the seam allowance about ¼" away from any bulky intersections. On this block, I clipped at the base of each Tri-Recs unit (where it met the center square unit). *Note:* see the Clipping Bulky Seam Allowances tutorial on page 75.

Sew the top and bottom rows to the center square unit, pressing the seams away from the center. The block should measure 13" square unfinished. Make 20 blocks.

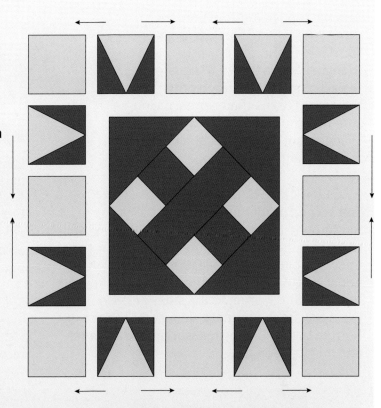

ASSEMBLING THE QUILT

Lay out your quilt blocks, sashing and 2 ½" background squares as shown. Sew the blocks and sashing together into rows. Press the seams toward the sashing strips. Sew the rows together. Press the seams toward the sashing.

BORDERS

FIRST BORDER
The first border for this quilt is made by sewing Tri triangles together, alternating the colors and "bookending" with brown Rec pieces. Make 2 side borders using 2 brown Rec triangles, 20 background Tri triangles and 19 brown Tri triangles. Press the seams toward the last piece sewn

Designer's Note: When you're ready to sew the borders to the quilt, do a little test to see which is longer – the quilt or the border. Whichever is longer needs to go on the bottom when you're sewing to help ease in the extra. I stay stitched approximately ⅛" along the edges of these borders to help minimize the stretch of each unit.

Stich the border to the side of the quilt, making sure that the wide end of the brown triangles are next to the blocks. Press the seam allowances toward the sashing.

IOWA SOIL BLOCK
MAKE 20
12 ½" FINISHED

Sew the top and bottom borders using 2 Rec triangles, 16 background Tri triangles and 15 brown Tri triangles. Sew a brown 4" square to each end of the border. Stitch the border to the quilt center, making sure that the wide ends of the brown triangles are next to the blocks. Press the seam allowances open.

SECOND BORDER

The second border uses the 5" x 82" strips of background fabric. Measure the quilt from top to bottom through the center and again at the midway points. If the measurements are not equal, calculate the average and cut 2 borders that size. Stitch them to the sides of the quilt. Press toward the borders. Repeat for the top and bottom borders, again measuring at the center and midway points.

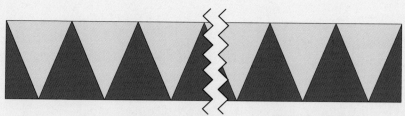

FIRST BORDER

FINISHING

BACKING
Piece the backing to about 81" x 95".

QUILTING
This top was custom quilted with diagonal lines across the blocks and feathers cascading from the border triangles.

BINDING
Make about 360" of binding using the brown strips. See the Binding tutorial on page 75 for instructions.

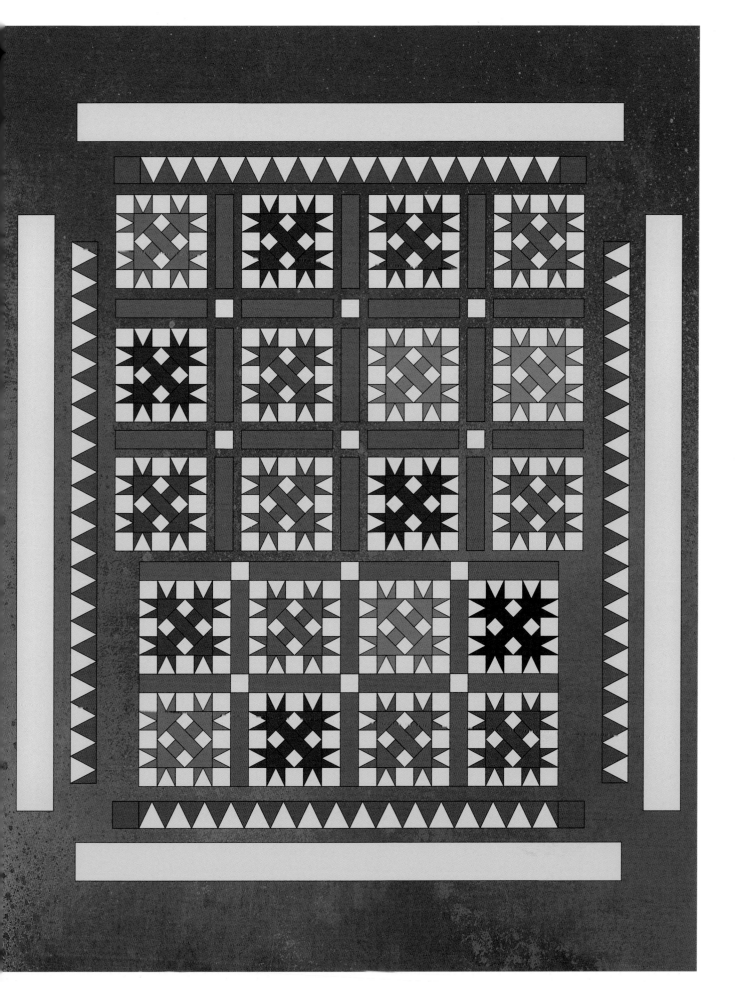

46 ½" x 55 ½"
Finished block size: 4 ½"

Made by
Joyce Dean Gieszler

Quilted by
Leanne Reid

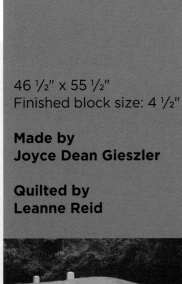

CIVIL STRIPES

This pattern was designed to use scraps from another project and to honor my great-grandfather's service in the Civil War. He told three lies to get into the Civil War – he lied about his age, the spelling of his name and where he lived. While he told three lies to get into the war, he said he would have told a thousand to get out!

This quilt uses strip piecing to mimic a string quilt and over-sized pieces to make the quarter-square triangles.

FABRIC AND SUPPLIES

2 ½ yards total assorted scrap prints for blocks
2 ¼ yards red prints for border blocks, outer borders and binding
¾ yard green print for inner border
⅜ yard gold print for inner border
3 yards print for backing

5" ruler, optional

CUTTING

ASSORTED SCRAP FABRICS
240 strips – 1 ¾" x 8"

GOLD
2 strips – 4" x the width of fabric. Subcut into 14 – 4" squares.

GREEN
- 4 strips – 2 ½" x the width of fabric
- 2 strips – 4" x width of fabric. Subcut into 14 – 4" squares.
- 2 – 3 ½" squares

RED
- 4 strips – 6" x 50" length of fabric for borders
- 3 strips – 4" x the width of fabric. Subcut into 28 – 4" squares.
- 2 – 3 ½" squares
- 6 strips – 2 ¼" x the width of fabric for binding

SEWING THE BLOCKS

For each block, you will need 5 scrap strips. Be sure each block contains a variety of prints and colors. Sew 5 strips together along the 8" side. Press all seams in one direction. Make 48 of these strips sets.

Place the 5" ruler as shown in the illustration, centering the ruler along the middle strip. Cut out 1 square per strip set.

Designer's note: Sometimes the strip sets are just narrow enough that there is a tiny piece missing from the corner of your cut block. No worries – it will be hidden in the seam allowance.

Or, cut 5" squares of freezer paper. Iron the freezer paper to the strip set on the diagonal, centering as illustrated above, and use a rotary cutter and ruler to cut out 48 blocks. The freezer paper may be used several times before it loses its "sticky."

If you love paper piecing, you could also use that method to make this block. A template is included here.

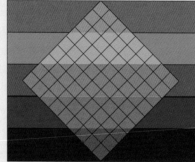

CIVIL STRIPES BLOCK
MAKE 48
5" UNFINISHED

OPTIONAL
PAPER PIECING
TEMPLATE

SEWING THE BORDERS

INNER BORDER

Draw a diagonal line on the wrong side of all the gold squares. Place 1 gold square and 1 red square right sides together. Sew ¼" on both sides of the drawn center line. Cut apart on the diagonal line. Open and press the triangles with seams toward the red fabric. This makes 2 half-square triangles. Make 28 gold/red half-square triangles. Repeat the above instructions to make 28 green/red half-square triangles.

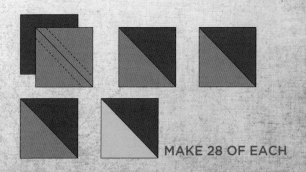

MAKE 28 OF EACH

Draw a diagonal line across the seam on the wrong side of each gold/red half square triangle. Layer 1 gold/red half square triangle and 1 green/red half square triangle, right sides together, with opposite color triangles together. Stitch ¼" from each side of the diagonal line. Cut apart on the diagonal line. Open and press the triangles with seams toward the red fabric. This makes 2 quarter-square triangles. Make 56 quarter-square triangles. Square each quarter-square triangle to 2 ¾". See the Squaring a Block or Unit tutorial on page 74 for instructions.

MAKE 56 OF EACH
2 ¾" UNFINISHED

CORNER BLOCKS FOR BORDER
Use the method described on page 37 to make 4 half-square triangles from 3 ½" red and green fabric for the corners. Square each half square triangle to 2 ¾".

QUILT ASSEMBLY

Lay out your quilt blocks in 8 rows of 6 blocks to see the overall effect and to balance colors. Sew the blocks together into rows, pressing the seams in one direction on odd-numbered rows and in the opposite direction on even-numbered rows. Press seams between the rows all in one direction.

BORDERS

FIRST BORDER
Sew 16 quarter-square triangles together to make the side borders as shown. Press the seams open between each quarter-square triangle. Stitch the borders to the quilt, ensuring that the gold triangles are next to the quilt center. Press the seams toward the quilt.

Sew 12 quarter-square triangles together to make the top and bottom borders. Sew 1 half-square triangle to each end of the top and bottom borders as shown. Press the seams open between each quarter-square triangle. Stitch the top and bottom borders to the quilt, again ensuring that the gold triangles are next to the quilt. Press the seams toward the quilt.

SECOND BORDER

The second inner border uses 2 ½" strips of green fabric. Measure the quilt from top to bottom through the center and again at the midway points. If the measurements are not equal, calculate the average and cut 2 borders that size. Stitch them to the sides of the quilt. Press toward the borders. Repeat for the top and bottom borders, again measuring at the center and midway points.

OUTER BORDER

Repeat border instructions for the outer border using 6" strips of red fabric. Measure the quilt from top to bottom through the center and again at the midway points. If the measurements are not equal, calculate the average and cut 2 borders that size. Stitch them to the sides of the quilt. Press toward the borders. Repeat for the top and bottom borders, again measuring at the center and midway points.

FINISHING

BACKING

Piece the backing to about 56" x 65".

QUILTING

This top was quilted with an allover design called Popcorn by Jodi Beamish of Willow Leaf Studio. Refer to Resources on page 79 for contact information.

BINDING

Make about 240" of binding using the red print strips. See the Binding tutorial on page 75 for instructions.

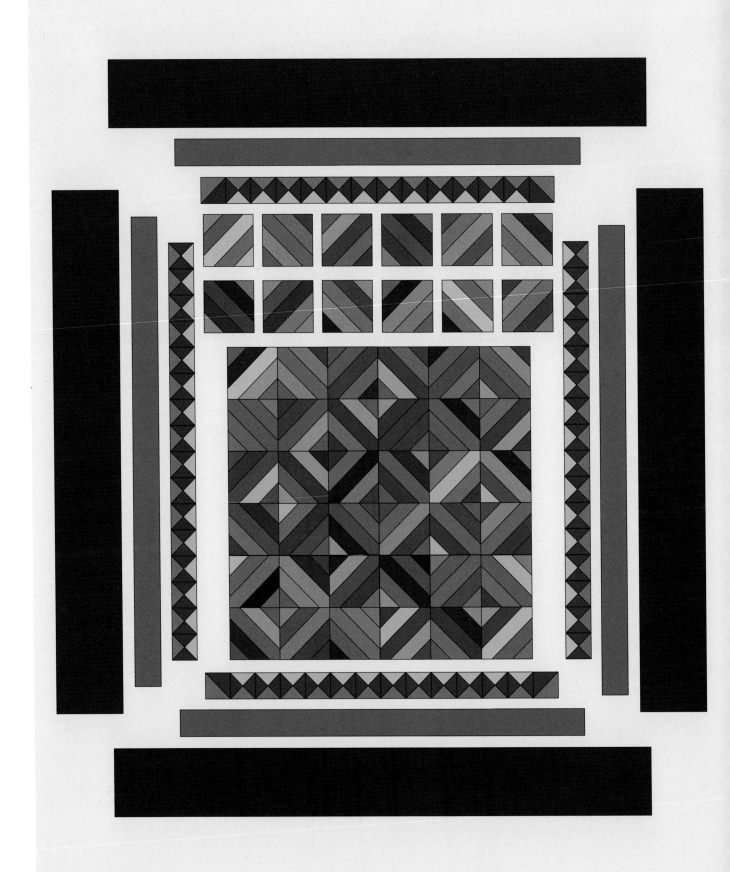

71" square
Finished block: 14"

**Made by
Joyce Dean Gieszler**

**Quilted by
Shawn Priggel**

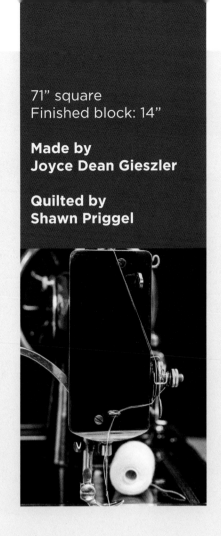

DIAMOND CROSS

Every year I teach a mystery quilt for my local guild. It's been a lot of fun coming up with new patterns for them that don't look alike. None of mine are one-day mysteries, and I see lots of finished projects every year. I looked through Maggie Malone's "5,500 Quilt Block Designs" book and found this Diamond Cross block. I knew it would be perfect for a mystery because it has so many pieces and parts and most of it is cut from 2 ½" strips. This is my third design using this block, and I love each one of them!

The Diamond Cross block was originally published by The Kansas City Star in 1937. This is a great quilt for learning to use the Tri-Recs Tool and Easy Angle ruler.

FABRIC AND SUPPLIES

3 ¾ yards gray print for blocks, borders and binding

1 ½ yards black print for blocks, sashing and borders

1 ¼ yards cream print for blocks and sashing

½ yard red print for blocks

4 ¾ yards for backing

Tri-Recs Tool

4 ½" or 6 ½" Easy Angle Ruler

CUTTING

Cutting is based on 40" wide fabric. See the Cutting with Specialty Rulers tutorial on page 79 for cutting instructions.

GRAY
1 – 72" length of fabric and subcut:
- 4 – 4 ½" x 72" pieces for inner borders
- 4 – 2 ½" x 72" pieces for outer borders
- 44 – 2 ½" x 6 ½" pieces

FROM THE REMAINING GRAY, CUT:
- 2 strips – 6 ½" x the width of fabric. Subcut into 28 – 2 ½" x 6 ½" rectangles (you need 72 total).
- 12 strips – 2 ½" x the width of fabric. Subcut 3 strips into 44 – 2 ½" squares and 8 pairs of Rec triangle pairs cut with the Tri- Recs tool. Be sure to fold the fabric strip right sides together so you have mirrored pairs. Reserve the remaining 9 strips for the gray and black half-square triangles border units.
- 8 strips – 2 ¼" x width of fabric for binding.

CUTTING CONT.

BLACK

18 strips – 2 ½" x the width of fabric. Subcut 52 – 2 ½" squares and 44 Tri pieces. Reserve 3 of the remaining strips for the black and cream half-square triangles and 9 strips for black and gray half-square triangles.

CREAM

15 strips – 2 ½" x the width of fabric. Subcut into 24 – 2 ½" x 14 ½" rectangles and 45 – 2 ½" squares. Reserve the remaining 3 strips for black and cream half-square triangles.

RED

5 strips – 2 ½" x the width of fabric. Subcut into 36 – 2 ½" x 4 ½" rectangles.

SEWING THE BLOCKS

HALF-SQUARE TRIANGLE UNITS

Layer a 2 ½" gray strip and a 2 ½" black strip right sides together. Using the Easy Angle Ruler, cut matched pairs of triangles. Repeat using 9 black and 9 gray strips to cut a total of 216 matched pairs of triangles. Sew along the diagonal. Press the seams toward the black.

Using the same method, cut and sew 72 cream and black half-square triangle units.

FOUR-PATCH UNITS

Watch the orientation of the half-square triangles. You want a "butterfly" to form in the center of the four-patch. Stitch a cream 2 ½" square to the right side of a cream and black half-square triangle. Press the seam allowance toward the cream square. Make 36. Next, stitch a gray 2 ½" square to the left side of a black and cream half-square triangle. Press the seam allowance toward the gray square. Make 36.

  MAKE 36 OF EACH

Sew the 2 halves together to make a butterfly four-patch. Press the seam open to reduce bulk. The four patches should measure 4 ½" square. Make 36.

BLOCK CENTER

Lay out the center of the block as shown. Stitch a butterfly four-patch on opposite sides of a red 2 ½" x 4 ½" rectangle. Watch the orientation to be sure the gray pieces are directly across from one another. Press the seam toward the red. Stitch a red 2 ½" x 4 ½" rectangle on either side of a cream 2 ½" square. Press the seams toward the rectangles. Sew the rows together, and press the seams toward the red rectangles. The center unit should measure 10 ½" square. Make 9.

BLOCK BORDERS

Lay 2 – 2 ½" x 6 ½" gray rectangles right sides together. Using the Recs tool, cut off the triangle at the right side and throw it away. Cut 36 pairs in this same manner.

Take 1 rectangle pair you just trimmed and lay them right sides up as shown. Sew a black Tri triangle to each side you just trimmed. Here's the magic of the Tri-Recs rulers: Place the blunt edge of the top of the Tri triangle so that it just touches each side of the triangle. Align the long edges as shown and stitch. Press the seams toward the rectangles. *Do not trim the dog ears.*

To sew the other side in the same manner, line up your dog ears and stitch. Press the seam away from the Tri triangle. Make 36. Now you can trim those dog ears. These pieces were made oversized and need to be trimmed to 10 ½" long. To do that, line up the 5 ¼" mark on your ruler with the center of the Tri triangle. Trim off one edge, turn and align the 5 ¼" mark and trim again.

Take 18 of the units you just made, and sew a black 2 ½" square to each end. Press the seams toward the Tri piece.

Stitch the side units first, then add the top and bottom units. Press the seams toward the Tri triangles. The block should measure 14 ½" square. Make 9.

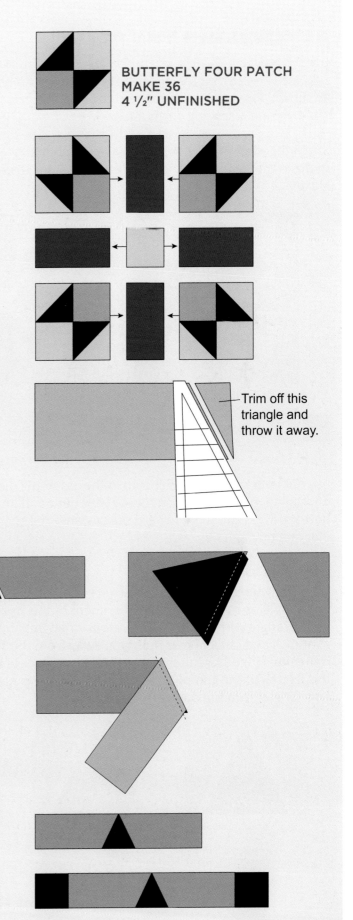

BUTTERFLY FOUR PATCH
MAKE 36
4 ½" UNFINISHED

Trim off this triangle and throw it away.

ASSEMBLING THE QUILT

SASHING

Sew a 2 ½" x 14 ½" cream rectangle sashing strip between the blocks as shown. Press the seams toward the sashing strips. Sew each row with 3 blocks and 4 sashing strips. Make 3.

Stitch together black 2 ½" squares and cream 2 ½" x 14 ½" rectangles to make the sashing as shown. Press the seams toward the rectangles. Make 4.

Lay out your quilt rows as shown in the assembly diagram. Sew a row of sashing in between each row of your quilt and one on the top and bottom. Press the seam toward the sashing. See the quilt assembly diagram on page 49.

SEWING THE BORDERS

With right sides together, lay one Recs triangle on the left side of the Tri triangle as shown. Note the alignment of the "magic angle" on the Recs triangle with the bottom of the Tri triangle. Align the long edges as shown and stitch. Press the seam away from the Tri triangle. With right sides together, stitch the second Recs triangle to the right side of the Tri triangle to complete the square. Press the seam away from the Tri triangle. Trim the dog ears. Make 8.

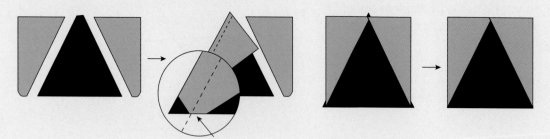

FIRST BORDER

The first border consists of 12 half-square triangles "leaning" toward the left, 1 Tri-Recs unit and 12 half-square triangles "leaning" toward the right. Refer to the quilt assembly diagram for placement. Press the seams away from the Tri-Recs unit. Make 4.

Designer's Note: This border could also be pressed all in one direction or with seams open.

When you're ready to sew the borders to the quilt, do a little test to see which is longer – the quilt or the border. Whichever is longer needs to go on the bottom when you're sewing to help ease in the extra. I stay stitched approximately ⅛" along the edges of these borders to help minimize the stretch of each unit.

Sew the borders to each side of the quilt center. Press the seams toward the quilt center. Stitch a gray 2 ½" square to each end of the 2 remaining borders before sewing to the quilt top and bottom. Press the seams toward the quilt center.

SECOND BORDER

Use the 4 ½" x 72" strips for this border. You'll be trimming them down to the correct length. Measure the quilt from top to bottom through the center and again at the midway points. If the are not equal, calculate the average and cut 2 borders that size. Stitch them to the sides of the quilt. Press toward the borders. Repeat for the top and bottom borders, again measuring at the center and midway points.

THIRD BORDER

The third border consists of 15 half-square triangles leaning to the left, one Tri-Recs unit and 15 half-square triangles leaning to the right. Refer to the quilt assembly diagram for placement. Make 4. Sew borders to each side of the quilt center. Press the seams toward the quilt center. Stitch a gray 2 ½" square to each end of the 2 remaining borders before sewing to the quilt top and bottom. Press the seams toward the quilt center.

FINAL BORDER

Sew in the same manner that you sewed the second border. Use the remaining 2 ½" x 72" strips for this border. Measure the quilt from top to bottom through the center and again at the midway points. If the measurements are not equal, calculate the average and cut 2 borders that size. Stitch them to the sides of the quilt. Press toward the borders. Repeat for the top and bottom borders, again measuring at the center and midway points.

FINISHING

BACKING
Piece the backing to about 80" x 80".

QUILTING
This top was custom quilted with straight stitching to emphasize the cross and tight curlicues in the sashing. The borders have diagonal sections with quilting in every other section.

BINDING
Make about 320" of binding using the gray print strips. See the Binding tutorial on page 75 for instructions.

Topper: 28" square
Runner: 19" x 64"
Finished block size: 12"

**Made by
Joyce Dean Gieszler**

**Quilted by Cheryl
Clements Ferris**

GRANDPA'S ALL STARS

Stars have been in quilts forever. They surround us, amaze us and comfort us. It's no wonder we continue to make quilt after quilt with stars! There were so few pieces in these small projects that I decided to go with simple math as my tool. Flying Geese are made by sewing squares to rectangles. It's a great project to use up scraps from Dad's plaid shirts, to give as a house-warming gift or to make in seasonal colors. I use the topper under the lamps on my end tables.

FABRIC FOR TOPPER

5 fat eighths assorted plaids for the stars and center square (blue, gray, orange, red and purple)

4 – ⅛-yard cuts assorted light neutral prints for the star backgrounds

⅜ yard medium neutral print for the split rails, four-patches and sashing

½ yard navy print for split rails, four-patches, sashing and binding

1 yard for backing

FABRIC FOR RUNNER

¼ yard red for stars

¼ yard light neutral print for the star backgrounds

⅝ yard medium neutral print for the split rails, four-patches and sashing

¾ yard blue for split rails, four-patches, sashing and binding

1 ½ yard for backing

CUTTING FOR TOPPER

ASSORTED PRINTS
From the blue, cut 1 – 3 ½" square of star fabric for the center of the topper

FROM EACH REMAINING PRINT, CUT:
- 1 – 3 ½" square
- 8 – 2" squares

ASSORTED LIGHT NEUTRALS
- For each star background, cut 1 strip – 2" x the width of fabric. Subcut strip into 4 – 2" x 3 ½" rectangles and 4 – 2" squares.

CUTTING CONT.

MEDIUM NEUTRAL
- 3 strips – 2" x the width of fabric
- 1 strip – 3 ½" x the width of fabric

NAVY
- 3 strips – 2" x the width of fabric
- 4 strips – 2 ¼" x the width of fabric for binding
- 32 – 3 ½" squares and cut 16 triangle shapes using the Tri Tool.
- 6 strips – 2" x the width of fabric
- 10 strips – 1 ½" x the width of fabric

RED
- 6 strips – 2" x the width of fabric
- 2 strips – 1 ½" x the width of fabric
- 6 strips – 2 ¼" x the width of fabric for the binding

CUTTING FOR RUNNER

ASSORTED PRINTS
FROM RED, CUT:
- 4 – 3 ½" squares
- 32 – 2" squares

LIGHT NEUTRAL
- 3 strips – 2" x the width of fabric. Subcut into 16 – 2" x 3 ½" rectangles and 16 – 2" squares.

MEDIUM NEUTRAL
- 3 strips – 2" x the width of fabric
- 3 strips – 3 ½" x the width of fabric. Subcut into 13 – 3 ½" x 6 ½" rectangles.

BLUE
- 3 strips – 2" x the width of fabric
- 1 strip – 3 ½" x the width of fabric
- 5 strips – 2 ¼" x the width of fabric for binding

SEWING THE BLOCKS FOR TOPPER AND RUNNER

FLYING GEESE UNITS

Draw a diagonal line on the wrong side of all 2" star squares. With right sides together, place a 2" square on the left side of a star background rectangle. Stitch a thread's width away from the drawn line, toward the upper left corner. Cut the seam allowance to ¼", and press the seam away from the rectangle. Repeat on the opposite corner, stitching a thread's width away from your drawn line, stitching on the side toward the upper right corner.

Make 16 units – 4 of each color for the Topper.

Make 16 red units for the Runner.

STAR POINT UNITS
MAKE 4
FOR EACH BLOCK

STARS

Each star is made of 4 – 2" background squares, 4 flying-geese units and 1 – 3 ½" center square. Lay out as shown in the diagram, and stitch into rows. Press the seams in the direction shown by the arrows. Stitch the rows together, pressing the seams toward the center of the block. The block measures 6 ½" square.

Make 4 assorted blocks for the topper.

Make 4 red blocks for the runner.

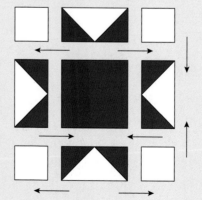 

STAR BLOCK
MAKE 4
6 ½" UNFINISHED

BLOCK SASHING – SPLIT RAILS

Stitch 2" strips of the star background and blue or navy fabrics together as shown. Press the seam toward the dark. The strip set measures 3 ½" wide. Make 3.
Cut into 16 – 6 ½" units of navy for the topper.
Cut into 16 – 6 ½" units of blue for the runner.

6½"

FOUR-PATCH UNITS

Stitch 2" strips of neutral sashing and blue or navy fabrics. Press the seam toward the dark. For the topper, make 3 strip sets. Cut into 32 – 2" units and 8 – 3 ½" units. Reserve the 3 ½" units for the top assembly. For the runner, make 4 strips sets and cut into 32 – 2" units and 16 – 3 ½" units. Reserve the 3 ½" units for the top assembly.

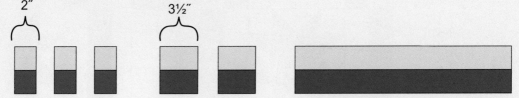

2"   3½"

Sew 4 – 2" units together to make 4 – four-patch units per block. Press the seams open.
Make 16 navy four-patch units for the topper.
Make 16 blue four-patch units for the runner.

Designer's Note: It's tempting to "spin" the four-patch centers, but pressing them open in this case will help them nest with the rest of the sashing.

STAR BLOCK ASSEMBLY

Each star block is made of 1 center star block, 4 split rail units and 4 four-patch units. Sew the star blocks together following the diagram. Press the seams toward the split rail unit.
Make 4 assorted star blocks for the topper.
Make 4 red star blocks for the runner.

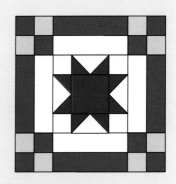

STAR BLOCK
MAKE 4
12 ½" UNFINISHED

SASHING FOR THE TOPPER

Sew a reserved 3 ½" unit to each end of a
3 ½" x 6 ½" medium neutral piece as shown
in the diagram. Press the seams toward the dark.
Make 4 sashing units for the topper.

ASSEMBLING THE TOPPER

Lay out the 4 blocks, sashing and red center sashing
square as shown in the diagram. Sew together in rows.
Press the seams open between the rows.

SASHING FOR THE RUNNER

Sew a reserved 3 ½" unit to each end of a 3 ½" x 6 ½"
medium neutral piece as shown in the diagram. Press
the seams toward the dark. Make 5 sashing units for
the runner.

54

VERTICAL SASHING FOR RUNNER

Referring to the diagram, sew together 1 – 3 ½" blue strip,
1 – 2" medium neutral strip and 1 – 2" blue strip. Press the seams
toward the dark. The strip set should measure 6 ½" wide.
Make 1. Subcut into 10 – 3 ½" units.

3½"

Sew 2 - 3 ½" units to either side of 1 neutral 3 ½" x 6 ½" strips as
shown in the diagram.

Lay out the 4 blocks and sashing units as shown. Sew together
in rows. Press the seams open between the rows.

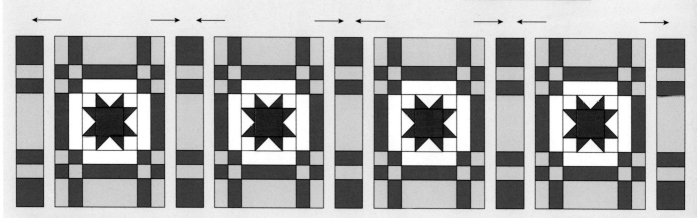

FINISHING

BACKING
TOPPER
Cut 1 – 36" x 36" square

RUNNER
Cut 2 pieces 27" x the width of fabric. Sew together along the
27" side. Trim to 72" long.

QUILTING
TOPPER

Grandpa's All Stars topper was quilted with cream-colored thread in a Continual Baptist Fan pattern by Hermione Agree of Urban Elementz. Refer to Resources, page 79, for contact information.

RUNNER

The runner was quilted using cream-colored thread in a Fork In the Road pattern by Barbara Becker of Urban Elementz. Refer to Resources, page 79, for contact information.

BINDING
TOPPER

Make about 160" of binding using the navy print strips for the Topper.

RUNNER

Make about 186" of binding using the blue print strips for the Runner. See the Binding tutorial on page 75 for instructions.

61" square
Finished block: 8"

**Made by
Joyce Dean Gieszler**

**Quilted by
Leanne Reid**

GRANDMOTHER'S JEWELS

A friend told me that when her grandmother passed away, her grandfather took his wife's costume jewelry and made kaleidoscopes for the grandchildren. I thought this was a great idea, and this quilt was born. The strips behind the pink stars remind me of the fractured sections of a kaleidoscope.

I wanted a rustic, folk look to this quilt and used straight-edge machine appliqué to sew the pink triangles. I borrowed garment construction techniques to make this easier and have also included instructions for fusible web. This quilt is a greatly simplified variation of a Spider Web pattern.

FABRIC AND SUPPLIES

2 ¼ yards pink (includes binding)

1 ¾ yards black

1 ½ yards gold

¾ yard purple

¾ yard blue

¾ yard red

¾ yard green

3 ¾ yards backing

4 ½" square ruler

Freezer paper

Spray starch or starch alternative, such as Best Press

Optional: 1 ⅞ yards of 17" wide Heat and Bond Lite

TEMPLATE

Trace the star point template found on page 62 onto freezer paper. You may want to make several copies. You will only need one copy if you're using fusible bond for star points.

CUTTING

PINK

- 7 - 2 ¼" strips x the width of fabric for the binding

- 4 strips – 6" x the length of fabric for borders

- Press the remaining fabric with starch or starch alternative to help stabilize it and cut into 4 ½" strips. Iron on the freezer paper templates, and cut with a rotary cutter. Only 2 edges of your star point will be on the bias. Cut 36.

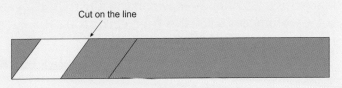
Cut on the line

CUTTING CONT.

Designer's Note: If you choose to make the star points with fusible bond, press a 17" x 65" piece of fusible bond onto the wrong side of the pink fabric, following the manufacturer's instructions. Trace around the template, and cut out 36 star points. Peel the paper backing off the star points. Set aside until it is time to add them to the quilt.

BLACK

- 5 – 1 ½" strips x the width of fabric for the inner border
- 24 – 2" strips x the width of fabric for the blocks

GOLD

24 – 2" strips x the width of fabric for the blocks

PURPLE

12 – 2" strips x the width of fabric for the blocks

BLUE

12 – 2" strips x the width of fabric for the blocks

RED

12 – 2" strips x the width of fabric for the blocks

GREEN

12 – 2" strips x the width of fabric for the blocks

SEWING THE BLOCKS

Sew together the 2" strips in sets of black, blue, gold and red. Press the seams **toward** the black strip. Make 12 strip sets.

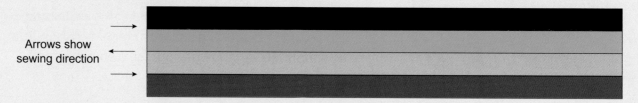

Arrows show sewing direction

Designer's Note: Starting the stitching at alternate ends prevents a curve from developing in your strip set.

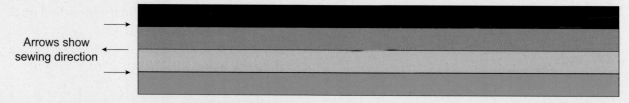

Arrows show sewing direction

Sew together the 2" strips in sets of black, purple, gold and green. Press the seams **away** from the black strip. Make 12 strip sets.

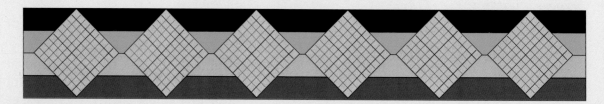

Place the 4 ½" ruler as shown in the illustration, centering the ruler along the center seam of the strip set. Carefully cut 6 squares from each strip set.

Designer's Note: The leftover triangles could be made into a doll quilt!

ASSEMBLING THE BLOCK

Sew 4 units together as shown to make 1 large block. Be sure that you have the red and green triangles meeting in the center. Press all seams open. Make 36.

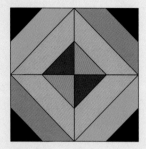

MAKE 36
8 ½" UNFINISHED

BASTING THE STAR POINTS

Designer's Note: If you chose to use fusible web for the star points, skip this basting step.

Set your machine for a long stitch length. If you normally use 2.0 or 2.5, change to 3.0 or 3.5. Change to thread that matches the diamond. Stitch a scant ¼" along each edge of the diamond. I chain stitched these and just went from one edge to the next. Finger press the diamonds by folding under the seam allowance to the wrong side, being sure to roll the stitching to the underside. Press with a dry iron. Make 36.

Your diamonds should measure approximately 8" long. A little longer is better than a little shorter. If the diamonds are too short, the points won't meet on the blocks. If you're not happy with the measurement, adjust the seam allowance at the points to make them a little smaller than ¼". Remember, you can always take out the stay stitching after you've sewn your diamonds onto the quilt, so it's okay if a little thread shows on the top.

TEMPLATE

A

ASSEMBLING THE QUILT

Lay out the blocks as shown. Sew into rows, pressing all seams open.

Stitch your lengths of 1 ½" black strips together to make the inner border. Sew to the quilt top to help stabilize the edges. Measure the quilt from top to bottom through the center and again at the midway points. If the measurements are not equal, calculate the average and cut 2 borders that size. Stitch them to the sides of the quilt. Press toward the borders. Repeat for the top and bottom borders, again measuring at the center and midway points.

STAR POINT APPLIQUÉ

Pin a row of diamonds to the quilt top as shown on page 64. Note that the diamond is placed between the first and second blocks. You can use a bit of glue stick to hold these in place. Follow the arrows for stitching in a "figure 8" pattern (shown in black and red). Use a straight stitch, and sew approximately ⅛" away from the edge of the diamond. Turn the quilt, and repeat for the remaining diamonds.

If you're using fusible webbing for the star points, line up each diamond carefully and fuse in place following the manufacturer's instructions. I recommend a narrow zigzag stitch for the edges, sewing in the same figure 8 as above.

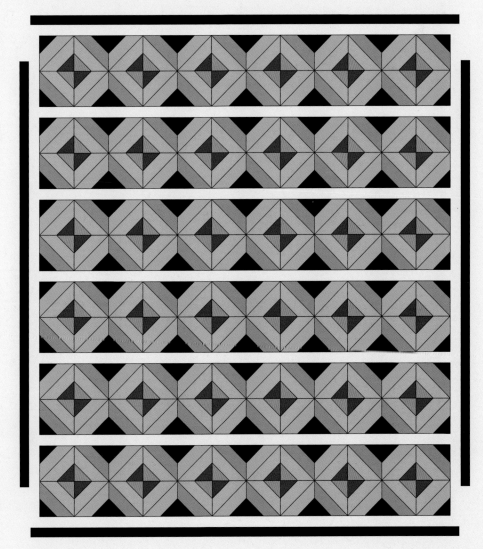

OUTER BORDER

The outer border uses the pink 6" x the length of fabric pieces you already cut. Measure the quilt from top to bottom through the center and again at the midway points. If the measurements are not equal, calculate the average and cut 2 borders that size. Stitch them to the sides of the quilt. Press toward the borders.
Repeat for the top and bottom borders, again measuring at the center and midway points.

FINISHING

BACKING
Piece the backing to about 67" x 67".

QUILTING
This top was custom quilted by Leanne Reid with flowers in each of the black squares, elongated swirls in the star points and large meandering filling in the rest.

BINDING
Make about 280" of binding using the pink strips. See the Binding tutorial on page 75 for instructions.

85" x 97"
Finished block: 10"

**Made by
Joyce Dean Gieszler**

**Quilted by Cheryl
Clements Ferris**

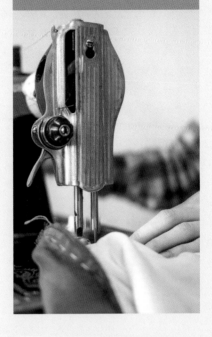

DUTCH FRIENDSHIP

I have always loved quilts with flying geese units, and many can be found made in fabrics from the Civil War era. I knew I wanted a scrappy quilt so began with cutting a couple of geese from any strips left over from other projects. My stack of geese began to grow while I worked on other quilts!

I've simplified the construction by using the Easy Angle and Companion rulers, with strips of fabric cut at 2 ½". This is a perfect quilt for swapping 2 ½" strips with friends. If you'd like a more controlled palette, consider making it from a Jelly Roll.

FABRIC AND SUPPLIES

3 yards total assorted prints for geese – a minimum of 39 – 2 ½" x 40" strips in a variety of purple, cheddar/yellow, gray, red, green, brown, pink and blue

2 ¾ yards gold print for wings and cornerstones

2 ½ yards black print for sashing and binding

2 ¾ yards cream print for sashing, friendship star and cornerstones

1 fat quarter red print for block centers

7 ½ yards for backing

BORDERS

3 ¾ yards if you have a directional fabric and want everything to face in the same direction (mine has birds)

OR 2 ½ yards of red print for borders cut the length of fabric

OR 1 ¾ yards of red print cut the width of fabric

4 ½" or 6 ½" Easy Angle ruler

Companion Angle ruler

CUTTING

See the Cutting with Specialty Rulers tutorial on page 72 for instructions.

ASSORTED PRINTS

Cut at least 39 strips – 2 ½" x the width of fabric. Using the Companion Angle ruler, cut 504 "geese." While you can cut 13 geese from each 40" strip of fabric, I recommend using up scraps and shorter strips to have a large variety of geese.

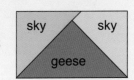

DUTCHMAN'S PUZZLE BLOCK EVOLUTION

I have always loved the Dutchman's Puzzle block and thought it would be fun to share the evolution of the block design, beginning with a traditional Dutchman's Puzzle and ending with the block for this quilt. As you can see, I went from Dutchman's Puzzle to Friendship Star. This quilt truly named itself!

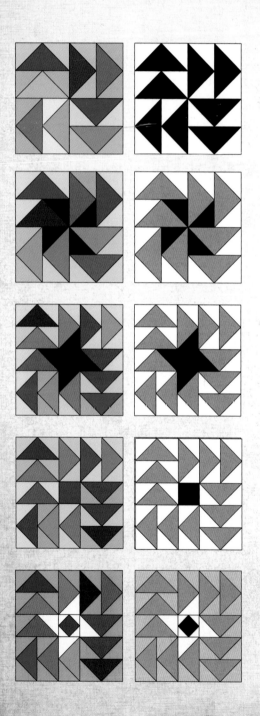

CUTTING CONT.

CREAM
- 7 strips – 2 ½" x the width of fabric for friendship stars. Set aside for cutting with the gold print strips.
- 5 strips – 2 ¼" x the width of fabric for the square-in-a-square units. Subcut into 84 – 2 ¼" squares, then cut each once on the diagonal.
- 50 strips – 1" x the width of fabric for sashing. If you have less than 42" of useable fabric in your strip, you'll need to cut 66 strips. There is enough fabric included in the yardage just in case.

BLACK
- 25 strips – 1 ½" x the width of fabric for sashing. If you have less than 42" of useable fabric in your strip, you'll need to cut 33 strips. There is enough fabric included in the yardage just in case.
- 10 strips – 2 ¼" x the width of fabric for binding
- 7 strips – 2 ¼" for the square-in-a-square units. Subcut into 112 – 2 ¼" squares, then cut each square once on the diagonal.

RED
- 2 strips – 1 ¾" x the width of fabric for the square-in-a-square units. Subcut into 42 – 1 ¾" squares.

GOLD
- 3 strips – 1 ¾" x the width of fabric for the square-in-a-square units. Subcut into 56 – 1 ¾" squares.
- 35 strips – 2 ½" x the width of fabric for wings. Set aside 7 strips for cutting with cream strips. Layer 2 gold strips right sides together, and cut 336 half-square triangle pairs using the Easy Angle ruler.

BORDERS
- For directional fabric, cut 2 – 6 ½" x 90" strips **and** 6 – 6 ½" x the width of fabric strips
- For one-piece borders, cut 4 strips – 6 ½" x the **length** of fabric
- For pieced borders, cut 9 strips – 6 ½" x the **width** of fabric strips

CUTTING THE FRIENDSHIP STAR UNITS
Layer the reserved 7 gold strips and 7 cream strips right sides together, with the cream strip on top. Cut 168 half-square triangle pairs using the Easy Angle ruler.

SEWING THE BLOCKS

FLYING GEESE UNITS

Align 1 half-square triangle piece on top of 1 goose piece with the top and side points matching. Stitch. Press the seam away from the goose. Repeat for the opposite side. For this quilt, I chain stitched in batches of 12. Make 168 with cream on the right and gold on the left to make the friendship star units. Make 336 additional geese units using gold on each side of the goose.

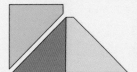  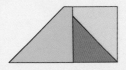 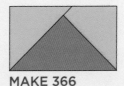

MAKE 366

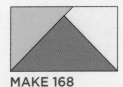

MAKE 168

SQUARE-IN-A-SQUARE UNITS

Mark the center of each side of the red squares with a small crease or pin. Sew a cream triangle to 2 opposite sides as shown. Press the seam toward the cream. Trim off the dog ears. Repeat with 2 more cream triangles. Trim block to 2 ½" square. At this point, you should just be sliver trimming. Sliver trimming is cutting a tiny bit of fabric from each side "just a sliver." I intentionally had the points of this block float just a bit to accommodate trimming.

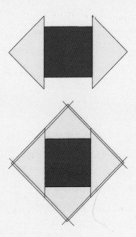

Note: See the Squaring a Block or Unit tutorial on page 74 for instructions.

Make 42 red/cream and 56 gold/black units.

SASHING

Stitch 1" strips of cream and 1 ½" black fabrics together as shown. Press the seams toward the center. The strip set should measure 2 ½" x the width of fabric. Make 25 strip sets. If your fabric had less than 42" of useable width, you will make 33 strip sets. Either way, cut into 97 – 10 ½" units as shown.

↓ 1″ cream

1½″ black

↑ 1″ cream

BLOCKS

Lay out each block in sections as shown. Sew sections together, pressing seams as shown by arrows. Make 42 blocks.

Designer's note: I do not press the center section seams until after I have sewn the block together. I check to be sure I'm happy with the points, then use a radical technique taught to me by a longarm quilter. I clip into the seam allowance on both sides of a bulky intersection, then press the block from the front, letting the seams on the back of the block fall naturally where they will. I always try to keep the seams away from the center square. See the Clipping Bulky Seam Allowances tutorial on page 75 for instructions.

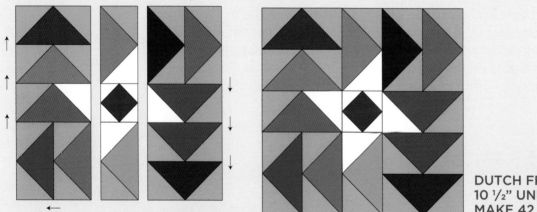

DUTCH FRIENDSHIP BLOCK
10 ½" UNFINISHED
MAKE 42

Lay out your quilt blocks, sashing and cornerstones as shown. Sew the blocks and sashing together into rows. Press all seams toward the sashing. Clip the seams as necessary to make the quilt lay flat.

BORDERS

If using directional fabric, be sure to make the orientation of the fabric all the same direction. In this case, all my birds are upright. For the top and bottom borders, sew strips along the 6 ½" side with a straight seam before stitching them to the quilt center. Measure the quilt from top to bottom through the center and again at the midway points. If the measurements are not equal, calculate the average and cut 2 borders that size. Stitch them to the sides of the quilt. Press toward the borders. Repeat for the top and bottom borders, again measuring at the center and midway points.

FINISHING

BACKING
Piece the backing to about 93" x 105".

QUILTING
Dutch Friendship was quilted with an allover feather pantograph called Whole Lotta Feathers by Patricia Ritter of Urban Elementz. Refer to Resources, on page 79, for contact information.

BINDING
Make about 400" of binding using the black strips. See the Binding tutorial on page 75 for instructions.

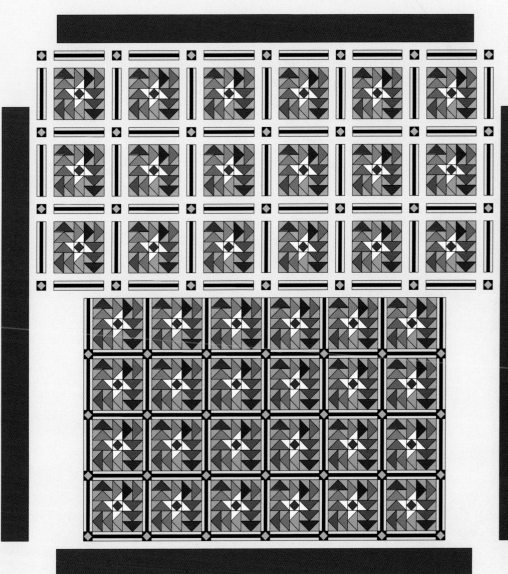

GENERAL CUTTING AND SEWING TUTORIALS

CUTTING WITH SPECIALTY RULERS

TRI-RECS TOOLS

Tri-Recs are my favorite tools for making triangle-in-a-square units, triangle borders and the Thousand Pyramids quilt pattern. One of the reasons I love specialty rulers so much is that they simplify the math for you. Figure out the finished size of your unit and add ½" for seam allowances. For example, if you want a 3" finished Tri-Recs unit, cut your strips at 3 ½".

To cut Tri triangles, lay the top edge of the tool along the top edge of the strip, and align the bottom of the strip with the corresponding line on the bottom of the tool (for example, the 2 ½" line for a 2 ½" strip of fabric). Cut on both sides of the tool. As you can see in the diagram, you then rotate the tool, align the top edge of the tool with the bottom of the strip and cut again.

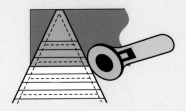 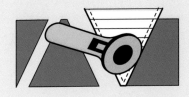

Note: It doesn't matter if your fabrics are right sides together or wrong sides together for this triangle. I stack mine up with four strips of fabric at a time.

To cut Recs triangles for Tri-Recs units, cut the same size strip for the Recs triangles as you did for the Tri triangles. Fold the strip right sides together to automatically cut both a right and a left triangle. I only cut through 2 thicknesses at a time when cutting this shape. Align the top of the tool with the top of the strip as shown. Cut as indicated. Trim off at the tip for the "magic angle." This will make alignment for piecing a breeze.

Magic angle

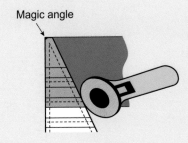

EASY ANGLE RULER

Line up the bottom of the tool along the edge of the strip, and slide it along the strip until the end of the strip fills the triangle area shown for the required size. The number corresponding to the strip width should be in the upper corner of the strip, as shown at the arrow on the diagram. The diagram shows a 2 ½" strip.

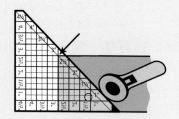

After cutting, flip the tool over, and line up the edge of the strips with that edge and the black triangle top of the tool below the strip as shown. Cut along the edge perpendicular to the strip. I usually stack up 4 strips if they are at least 2 ½" wide. I stack up less if the strips are narrower than that.

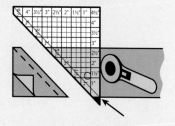

COMPANION ANGLE RULER

Cutting with the Companion Angle ruler is done exactly the same as the Tri-Recs tool. Stack up four strips at a time, line up the ruler along the top and bottom of the strip and cut. Flip the tool over, line up and cut again.

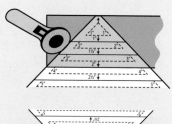

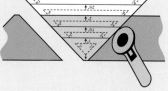

ALL KALEIDOSCOPE RULERS

Cutting with the kaleidoscope ruler is just the same as the Tri-Recs tool above. The difference is the degree of the angle of each ruler.

SQUARING A BLOCK OR UNIT

Sometimes a block or unit is sewn over-sized and needs to be cut down. This is called "squaring up a block." A perfect example is the quarter-square triangles made in the Civil Stripes pattern on page 34. To square these units to 2 ¾", use a small ruler – 6 ½" square or smaller with at least one diagonal line – and align the diagonal on your diagonal seam. One half of 2 ¾" is 1 ⅜" and this is the center of your block – where the 1 ⅜" horizontal and the 1 ⅜" vertical lines meet.

Square up these lines at the center of your block, and trim on two sides.

Rotate the block, and align the bottom and left side of the block on the 2 ¾" lines on the ruler. Trim the remaining two sides. Voila! A perfect 2 ¾" square.

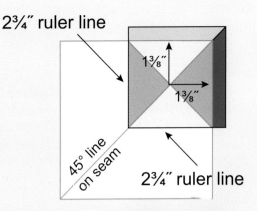

2¾″ ruler line

1³⁄₈″

1³⁄₈″

45° line on seam

2¾″ ruler line

This works for any block. Determine the size your block needs to be and divide that measurement in half. For example, for a 12 ½" finished block, the center would be at 6 ¼".

Here's a math chart to help you convert those fractions to marks on the ruler:

2¾″ square

.125	⅛"
.250	¼"
.375	⅜"
.500	½"
.625	⅝"
.750	¾"
.875	⅞"

CLIPPING BULKY SEAM ALLOWANCES

Sometimes the intersection of quilt blocks gets very bulky. I like to clip on each side of that intersection to help seams lay flat. Using just the tips of very sharp scissors, clip up to the seam line through all layers of the seam allowance. The clips are approximately ¼" away from each side of a seam intersection. Here is an example of how the clipping was used in the Dutch Friendship pattern.

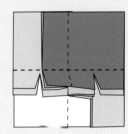
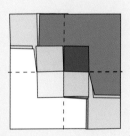

BINDING THE QUILT

I like to use narrow binding on all quilts, usually 2 ¼".

Join the 2 ¼" strips of binding fabric perpendicular to each other with right sides together. Stitch a seam across the diagonal. Check to ensure your seam creates one long length of binding before trimming the seam allowance to ¼". Press all seam allowances open to reduce bulk.

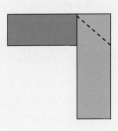

Fold the binding strip in half with wrong sides together. Press, being careful not to stretch the binding.

I recommend using a walking foot to sew on the binding. It helps to keep the layers from shifting. Measure in ¼" from each corner edge on the quilt. Mark with a pencil or pin. Before beginning to sew, choose a starting point other than a corner of the quilt. Lay out the binding loosely to make sure that when you sew the binding on, a seam will not fall at the corner.

Place the binding on the quilt approximately where you want the final binding seam to appear. Secure with one pin that is 2 ¼" from the cut edge of the binding. Place a second pin 8" from the cut edge of the binding and a third pin 8" to the left of the binding.

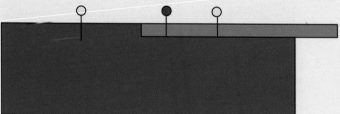

Match the raw edges of the binding with the raw edge of the quilt. Begin stitching at the pin on the far right. Sew a ¼" seam through all layers. For mitered corners, stop stitching ¼" from the corner, at the point you marked, backstitch and remove quilt from the sewing machine (A).

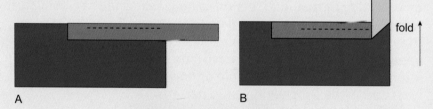

A   B   fold ↑

Rotate the quilt, and fold the binding straight up, away from the corner, forming a 45-degree angle (B). Bring binding straight down in line with the raw edge you're getting ready to sew, leaving the fold of fabric even with the raw edge you just finished. Begin stitching at the top edge, and continue down the side of the quilt to the next corner (C).

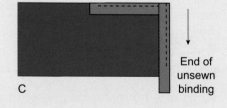

C   End of unsewn binding

Continue around the quilt until you reach the pin that is approximately 8" from the beginning of the binding. Backstitch to secure. Remove the quilt from the machine, and lay it flat so the unstitched binding is on top.

Take the binding on the left and gently stretch it toward the pin. Mark the intersection, with a pencil or chalk line, where the binding overlaps the pin. Cut the **ending** binding on the marked line. Note: Be sure not to cut the beginning binding that you already stitched down.

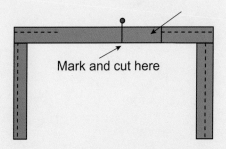

Mark and cut here

Place the binding strips perpendicular to each other as you did when making the binding, with right sides together. Pin in place. Before stitching across the diagonal, be sure to check that the binding will lie flat on the quilt. Stitch on diagonal line. Trim seam allowance to ¼". Finger press the seam open. Refold the binding, and align the raw edges of the binding with the raw edge of the quilt. Stitch in place.

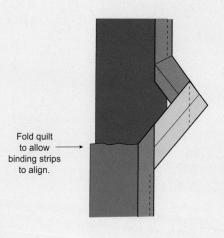

Fold quilt to allow binding strips to align.

Bring the folded edge of the binding to the quilt back. Blind stitch the folded edge to the quilt backing, being sure to cover the machine stitches.

78

RESOURCES

SPECIALTY RULERS AND PRODUCTS

EASY ANGLE AND COMPANION ANGLE RULERS
EZ Quilting by Wrights
(800) 660-0416
Email: help@wrights.com
www.ezquilt.com

THE TRIANGLER
(320) 796-0431
www.ankastreasures.bigcartel.com/product/the-triangler

QUILTSENSE TRIANGLE RULER
(800) 558-3568
www.frommarti.com

BEST PRESS
(800) 328-6294
www.maryellenproducts.com

CREATIVE GRIDS
1/4" Template Plastic (8" x 11") Item CGRTP14
www.creativegridsusa.com

QUILTERS

CHERYL CLEMENTS FERRIS
Hillsboro, Oregon
www.creativeheartsquilting.com

SHAWN PRIGGEL
Durham, North Carolina
Email: sppriggel@yahoo.com

QUILTING DESIGNS
Jodi Beamish, Willow Leaf Studio
(888) 945-5695
www.willowleafstudio.com

PATRICIA E. RITTER, URBAN ELEMENTZ
HERMIONE AGEE, URBAN ELEMENTZ
BARBARA BECKER, URBAN ELEMENTZ
125 Sunny Creek
New Braunfels, Texas 78132
(830) 964-6133
Email: patricia@urbanelementz.com
www.urbanelementz.com

SWEET DREAM QUILT STUDIO
2515 Basswood Court
Columbia, Missouri 65203
(573) 446-0421
Email: sweetdreamsqs@aol.com
www.sweetdreamquiltstudio.com

ABOUT THE AUTHOR

Joyce's life-long love affair with sewing began when she was four years old. She told her mother she knew why the sewing machine was called a Singer – because it hummed! She took sewing in home economics, but didn't really begin to love sewing clothes until she was in her early 20s. Joyce began her sewing career tailoring men's suits in the Portland, Oregon, area. After a move to Waco, Texas, she found a quilt shop inside of a converted carriage house. It was love at first sight! Several moves (California and Florida) and two children later, Joyce's love affair with quilts was firmly planted.

THEN AND NOW

One of the greatest joys of quiltmaking for Joyce is helping students recognize their talent and instilling in them a love of quilting. Her favorite times are when a student, of any age, insists they cannot be successful. The more skeptical, the better! She hasn't met a student yet that couldn't be successful given enough different ways to sew the same unit.

Photo by Katie Gieszler.

Joyce has been teaching quilting for 15 years and designing quilt patterns for 10. She began teaching by volunteering at a local alternative school and taught teen moms to make quilts for their babies. Joyce was honored to be the featured quilter at a show in her adopted hometown of Hillsboro, Oregon (95,000 residents). Joyce and her husband, Mike, are the proud parents of two adult children and a lovely daughter-in-law who joined the family in 2011.

Follow Joyce on her blog at www.quilterchickdesigns.com or join her Quilterchick Designs Facebook page. On her blog, you will find numerous tutorials that will help you make quilts faster and more accurate.